For it is not enough to have a good mind; the main thing is to apply it well.[1]

FSC
www.fsc.org
MIX
Papier aus ver-
antwortungsvollen
Quellen
Paper from
responsible sources
FSC® C105338

Bibliographic Information held by the German National Library: The details of the original German edition of this publication are held by the German National Library as part of the German National Bibliography; detailed bibliographical data can be found online at www.dnb.de.

© 2022 Dr Walther Ziegler
1st Edition July 2022
Jacket design and graphic design for the whole book: Silke Ruthenberg, making use of illustrations by:
Raphael Bräsecke, Creactive – Studio for Advertising, Comics & Illustrations
© JackF - Fotolia.com (image-frames)
© Valerie Potapova - Fotolia.com (image-frames)
© Svetlana Gryankina - Fotolia.com (speech-balloons)

Publisher and Printing:
BoD – Books on Demand, Norderstedt
ISBN 9-783-7562-1316-0

Walther Ziegler

Descartes
in 60 Minutes

Translated by
Alexander Reynold

My thanks go to Rudolf Aichner for his tireless critical editing; Silke Ruthenberg for the fine graphics; Lydia Pointvogl, Eva Amberger, Christiane Hüttner, and Dr. Martin Engler for their excellent work as manuscript readers and sub-editors; Prof. Guntram Knapp, who first inspired me with enthusiasm for philosophy; and Angela Schumitz, who handled in the most professional manner, as chief editorial reader, the production of both the German and the English editions of this series of books.

My special thanks go to my translator

Dr Alexander Reynolds.

Himself a philosopher, he not only translated the original German text into English with great care and precision but also, in passages where this was required in order to ensure clear understanding, supplemented this text with certain formulations adapted specifically to the needs of English-language readers.

Contents

Descartes' Great Discovery

The French thinker René Descartes (1596-1650) is one of the best-known philosophers in the world. His brief but renowned proposition "I think, therefore I am." is still today a compulsory part of every young French boy or girl's education. But above and beyond France, his ideas have surely become part of all humanity's cultural heritage. He is seen as the founder of Rationalism and thereby, in a sense, as father of the whole of modern philosophy. He surely deserves this honorific title because what Descartes dared to do, intellectually, was, in his day, something quite revolutionary. He is rightly called "the Columbus of philosophy". Just as the great seafarer discovered a hitherto unknown continent, the so-called "New World", Descartes succeeded in opening up a new dimension of knowledge and in changing our whole perspective on the world. Before Descartes, people in the Christian Western world had believed, for well over a millennium, in the words of the prophets, quite especially in Jesus Christ, and in the Bible as written testimony of divine revelation. For all these years, all knowledge about the cosmos, and about inner and outer Nature, had had its source and basis ultimately in religious faith.

Then came Descartes with a radical new demand. Truth, he claimed, ought no longer to consist in the supposed "revealed truth" of prophets and saints but should henceforth be based upon some sure and incontestable knowledge about the experienceable world. Because the theologians of the Middle Ages, Descartes insisted, had held far too many self-contradictory views about what was true or false. Although Descartes had been raised and educated as a good Roman Catholic, at an eminent school and college run by Jesuits, the most loyally orthodox of Christian religious orders, he had begun, so he tells his readers in retrospect, very early on to have doubts about all that he was being taught and learning. The very first, indeed, of his famous *Meditations on First Philosophy* opens with the words:

Some years ago I was struck by the large number of falsehoods that I had accepted as true in my childhood [...].[2]

But it was not just among the priests and theologians who had given him his education that Descartes discovered „falsehoods" and self-contradictory notions. These he found also among philosophers:

Regarding philosophy, I shall say only this: [...] that it has been cultivated for many centuries by the most excellent minds [...] yet there is no point in it which is not disputed and doubtful [...].[3]

There had been, then, so argued Descartes, not one single proposition in the whole of philosophy, from ancient times up to Descartes' own day, which had really stood the test of time. Lacking throughout, in other words, had been anything like a sure and incontestable knowledge. It was precisely the challenge of acquiring such a knowledge that Descartes now planned to take up. He planned the far from modest undertaking of creating once and for all a sure and certain body of truths, a starting point for genuine knowledge whose validity no one would be able to contest. In his own words, he set out to find that often-evoked "Archimedean point" from which it will prove possible for us to comprehend, assess and govern all the other things that make up our world and our universe:

> Archimedes used to demand just one firm and immovable point in order to shift the entire earth; so I too can hope for great things if I can manage to find just one thing, however slight, that is certain and unshakeable.[4]

Descartes embarked on a quest, then, for that which is certain and unshakeable. He himself judged this to be the noblest and most important task a philosopher could undertake. Once a firm and true ground and foundation for human knowledge had been found, everything else would follow naturally and spontaneously from this:

Thus, the whole of philosophy is like a tree. The roots are metaphysics, the trunk is physics, and the branches emerging from the trunk are all the other sciences [...][5]

Like many of the great philosophers of his day Descartes was a man skilled in a whole range of arts and sciences. Besides being a philosopher, he was also a pioneering mathematician and researcher in the natural sciences. Thus, many of us may remember from our school geometry lessons the so-called "Cartesian coordinate system" with its horizontal x- and vertical y-axis. But for Descartes the first and most fundamental thing that geometry, and indeed all the other individual "exact sciences" such as arithmetic and physics, needed and required was a firm basis for claims to knowledge. He poses, then, first and foremost the basic question: how does one arrive at certain knowledge? On what can I really rely: on what I see, hear and feel? On my reasoning and on logic itself? Or perhaps on what has been taught me from earliest childhood on? Descartes' radical answer to these questions runs: I can rely on nothing at all! I must begin by putting absolutely everything into question:

I realized that it was necessary once in the course of my life to demolish everything and start again right from the foundations if I wanted to establish anything at all in the sciences that was stable and likely to last.[6]

At this point Descartes did something quite unusual. In order indeed to "demolish everything" in the way of likely "falsehoods" that he had learned in his childhood and youth and to "start again right from the foundations", he withdrew, for a whole week, to a remote location and began to meditate. Hence the title of his principal work, which was to make him famous all over Europe: *Meditations on First Philosophy*. In this book, published in 1641, Descartes records step by step, as if in a personal journal, all the considerations that came to his mind in his search for a reliable criterion of truth. The book consists of no less than six successive "meditations" marking the stations on his way to the acquisition of an absolutely certain knowledge. Today, indeed, we tend to associate the word "meditation" mostly with those techniques of mental concentration derived from the Far East which help us to guide our attention and perception in such a way as to achieve an inner liberation from our involvement in the stress and strain of daily life. It was through meditation of this type, engaged in under a fig tree in the open air, that the Buddha, for example, arrived at his experience of "nirvana". But what Descartes means by "meditation" is something rather closer to the original sense of the Latin word *meditatio*: namely, "the finding of a centre or a middle". The "centre or middle" that Descartes wants to find out in his own meditations is not "the meaning of life" but rather that deepest and most inescapable knowledge upon which all other knowledge must be built:

[…] I will proceed in this way until I recognize something certain […].[7]

In sharp contrast to the Buddha, indeed, Descartes's meditations were not conducted in the open air and in the cross-legged posture of the yogi but rather seated in a bourgeois armchair set in front of a comfortable fireplace. In a way much like the Buddha, however, he began his meditations by attempting to free himself, there in the remote dwelling that he had retreated to, from all attachments and prejudices that he had brought along with him from the wider and more agitated world. This taking leave, indeed, and distancing of himself from all those learned beliefs and convictions which he had formerly held to be true had the result, as he confesses, of tipping him into a state of deep disorientation:

It feels as if I have fallen unexpectedly into a deep whirlpool which tumbles me around so that I can neither stand on the bottom nor swim up to the top.[8]

The highly personal and emotional language and imagery used in this passage is a clear indication in itself that, with Descartes, a new intellectual era has begun. He describes his key philosophical notion, and the path by which he has arrived at it, no longer in the cold intellectual language of the "philosophers of the schools" but rather in the literary style of an autobiographical novel or, as we have said, a personal diary or journal. This is as much a novelty as is his decision, in 1647, to publish the *Meditations* also in a French-language version, since in Descartes' lifetime it was still the general practice to publish philosophical works in Latin and in Latin alone. The readers such books were aimed at had been, up to this point, the Latin-speaking cultural elite and no one else. But Descartes expressly declares his intention of trying to alter this:

And if I am writing in French, my native language [...], it is because I expect that those who use only their natural reason in all its purity will be better judges of my

opinions than those who give credence only to the writings of the ancients.[9]

Descartes' expectation was not disappointed. His *Meditations on First Philosophy* made him famous in his own lifetime and went down in history, indeed, as an epoch-making work which still engages thinkers and writers even today. Descartes takes us, through the six short chapters making up this book, into the fascinating world of his own search for truth, so that we ourselves feel that we are being drawn into Descartes' "whirlpool" of analytical pondering over all those of aspects of our daily life and experience which are perhaps, at bottom, no more than imagination and illusion. In order to attain to some final certainty, Descartes argues, we need a radically new method – the method of systematic doubt:

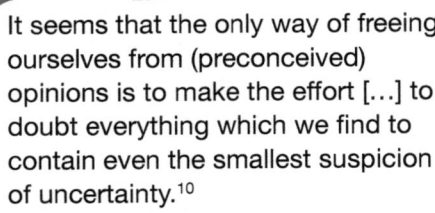

It seems that the only way of freeing ourselves from (preconceived) opinions is to make the effort [...] to doubt everything which we find to contain even the smallest suspicion of uncertainty.[10]

Thus, Descartes undertakes to doubt even what we see with our own eyes. Because this too may be an optical illusion or will o' the wisp. Even if we feel absolutely certain that we have perceived something correctly and accurately, the thing perceived could still prove not to be real. Because what assures us, for example, that we are not dreaming when we perceive and affirm in this way? Is there really anything, asks Descartes, that it is absolutely impossible to doubt? The answer which he eventually found to this question has become one of the most famous propositions in our modern culture:

[...] I am thinking, therefore I exist [...].[11]

Descartes' reasoning here ran as follows: I can doubt and call into question absolutely everything that I see and perceive around me, with the sole exception of the fact that, in this very moment when I am doubting and calling into question, I myself, the doubter and questioner, am alive to do so. If I doubt, then this means that I myself exist: a fact which remains unaltered regardless of whether I am in error, asleep, dreaming, or whatever else. Now, doubting is certainly, whatever else it is, also a form of thinking, so that the act of doubting itself necessarily generates Descartes' famous indubitable proposition which, given its full formulation in the *Discourse on Method*, runs:

[...] Observing that this truth 'I am thinking, therefore I exist' was so firm and sure that all the most extravagant suppositions of the sceptics were incapable of shaking it, I decided I could accept it without scruple as the first principle of the philosophy I was seeking.[12]

And this final – or, more properly speaking, initial and principal – certainty did indeed become the starting point for the whole of Descartes' philosophy. Because Descartes recognizes that "thinking" is precisely what is most essential to, and definitive of, a human being:

> Thought: this alone is inseparable from me [...] I am, then, in the strict sense, only a thing that thinks; that is, I am a mind, or intelligence, or intellect, or reason [...].[13]

This being the case, human beings should accept as "knowledge" only claims and propositions which are clear and logical. This applies to observations and theories on all topics, even on the topic of God. Even the existence of God, Descartes says, is something one ought, initially, to cast into absolute doubt. In a second step or stage, indeed, one can subject the possibility of this existence to a rational examination and testing and may, where reason appears to dictate it, accept this existence as proven after all. But by adopting this line of argument Descartes was taking a highly perilous stance. He himself was fully aware that putting knowledge in the place of blind belief in this way was, in the age that he lived in, a very risky undertaking. Early on in his career in 1633 he had been on the very point of publishing an important statement of his views not just on philosophy but on related natural-scientific questions when he received the news of Galileo's condemnation for heresy in Rome. Galileo had had to publicly recant his own astronomical views, involving the claim that the earth turned on its own axis, in order to avoid being put to death. Even after the recantation, although he escaped being burned at the stake, he was condemned to lifelong imprisonment. Since the views expounded in the work Descartes was about to published converged in many respects with Galilieo's, he had very good reason to fear a similar fate. He decided, therefore, not to publish this his first substantial work and even destroyed several chapters of it altogether. His *Discourse on Method*, published anonymously four years later in 1637, was an abbreviated and much more cautious statement of some, but not all, of the 1633 work's themes.[14]

Finally, at the age of forty-five, in the hope of being able to publish safely under his own name, he began to try to come to some sort of public accommodation with the church authorities. *The Meditations on First Philosophy*, which he publishes at this age, not only contain a lengthy "proof of God's existence"; they are even dedicated to

Those most learned and distinguished men [...] of the sacred Faculty of Theology at the University of Paris.[15]

By dedicating in this way his principal work to the theologians of the university, and laying it, as it were, voluntarily before them for their approval, Descartes hoped to avoid becoming himself the target of that charge of heresy brought against other intellectuals of his day and to be tolerated as he pursued his philosophical endeavours. Already on the very first page of the *Meditations* Descartes assures his readers that he is a firm believer in divine revelation. He also assures all those preparing to read him that the rational proof of God which he is about to offer, and which offers purely logical grounds for holding that there must be a God, is in his own case something entirely unnecessary, since he firmly believes in God even without such a logical proof. This "rational proof of God's existence", he says, is needed, if it is needed at all, only as a means of converting the "unbelievers" to whose class he did not belong:

[…] For us who are believers, it is enough to accept on faith that the human soul does not die with the body, and that God exists; but

in the case of unbelievers it seems that there is no religion […] that they can be persuaded to adopt until these two truths are proved to them by natural reason.[16]

The logical proof of God's existence that Descartes offers in the *Meditations* is, indeed, considered in retrospect a fascinating and exciting one. He tries to prove God's existence to be a necessary premiss of all rational thought by combining together the strongest proofs and arguments offered by his predecessors in this enterprise, such as Aristotle and the early-medieval Church Father Anselm of Canterbury. But in the end Descartes' attempt fails in two respects. Firstly, he is unable to prove the existence of God in a way which is really free of every logical fallacy. Secondly, he is unable to convince the theologians that his philosophy really is the "God-fearing" one they insist on. In the view of these theologians, indeed, no truly devout thinker would have called the existence of God into question in the first place, so that this existence would then have to be propped up and re-established by logical arguments. Contrary to his expectations, and although he had now withdrawn from France and settled in Calvinist Holland, the most liberal country in Europe at the time, Descartes found himself, for the rest of his life, forced constantly to defend and justify his own right to philosophize. A few years after his death his writings were banned both by the Pope and by the state censorship authorities of many countries. The French king, in particular, insisted on banning the sale and reading of his works.

Even censorship, however, could not prevent his key demand that knowledge henceforth be subject to the test of science and reason from spreading like wildfire round all the civilized world. Descartes' philosophy only ever set itself one paramount goal, namely:

[…] A true and certain knowledge.[17]

On his way to this goal Descartes discovered that his own thought and meditation, or in other words his own "I", played an absolutely decisive role in this whole question. It is, after all, always "I" who thinks – always "I" who, through this thinking, comprehends the world and gives to it shape and order. Since this discovery of Descartes' philosophy as a whole has become, and remained, a "reflexive" enterprise. That is to say, philosophy began no longer to ask just about the world it wished to understand but recognized now that to want to know about the world and "how the world is" is necessarily at the same time to want to know about the "knower" of this world, about the mind that asks questions about it. In other words, it is to want to know about one's own self. Are, for example, the questions which we ourselves pose to reality correctly and expediently formulated questions? Is the specific way in which we human beings ask and enquire about the world one which is apt to lead to a sure and certain knowledge?

Ever since Descartes, we have said, mankind has been searching for reliably precise methods of acquiring firm knowledge. But we have now noted that this is not possible except where we critically examine our own subjective procedures in thinking and knowing and reveal very clearly the premisses and presuppositions of these procedures. In this way there came into being a new science: the theory of knowledge, also called "epistemology". Regardless of whether one held, along with Descartes himself and the so-called "Rationalists" who followed directly in his footsteps, that true and precise knowledge was to be acquired by the application of pure reason and pure logical rules, or whether one held, as did the rival school of "Empiricists", that it was to be acquired rather through material sense and experience, governed and organized through experiments, one basic principle now applied to every enquirer into truth. One was obliged, henceforth, to give an account of just *how* one had arrived at the knowledge one claimed to be true, whatever this knowledge and this truth happened to be.

But it did not follow from the core idea expounded by Descartes just that Man needs to recognize himself to be an actively thinking being and thus to apply the clearest possible methods in seeking after truth. This idea also involved one further supposition: namely, that human thinking was something fundamentally distinct from every other phenomenon making up the world:

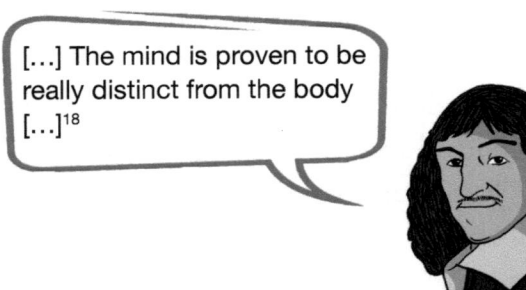

[…] The mind is proven to be really distinct from the body […][18]

Descartes distinguishes between two so-called "substances". These are a "thinking substance" on the one hand and a soul-less and mind-less "extended substance" on the other – or, to use the Latin terms actually used by Descartes, *res cogitans* and *res extensa*. There fall, for Descartes, under the category of *res extensa*, or "extended substance", such things as mineral and other matter, plants, animals and even our own human bodies. The *res cogitans*, for its part, or in other words our thinking capacity, can help us to understand and control that external world of material bodies, including our own, which at first confronts us as something entirely alien and "other" to us. All we need in order to do this is a correct application of thinking reason:

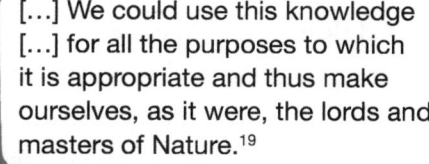

[…] We could use this knowledge […] for all the purposes to which it is appropriate and thus make ourselves, as it were, the lords and masters of Nature.[19]

This splitting of our universe into thinking on the one hand and a purely material external world on the other soon acquired the name "Cartesian dualism". It has continued to exert a decisive influence on Western consciousness ever since. Man, the "thinking subject", probes into and masters, in his capacity as *homo sapiens*, that "object" by which he finds himself constantly confronted. This "object" is Nature, and through mastering it Man makes Nature serve his ends. But, like many great philosophical contentions, this splitting of the world into subject and object, mind and matter, soulless and ensouled, has had consequences that are worrying as well as to be welcomed.

Is "thinking" really the most essential, and sole decisive, characteristic of what it is to be a human being? And does the world really consist in nothing but thought inside us and a soul-less, mind-less sphere of "bodies" outside of our minds? Must animals, for example, as Descartes supposes, really be classed among the *res extensa*, that is to say, be treated as mere "things"? Is it really the task of science to know matter, plants, animals and even the human body just as one would know and comprehend a "thing" and thus to subjugate these "things" to science's ends? What advantages and disadvantages arise therefrom? And above all: what can still count, today, as "true knowledge"?

Descartes is more than just a thinker who prepared the way for modern science. In a sense, we may say, his thinking became our culture's and our civilization's destiny. This is the case, as we shall see, in both a positive and a negative sense.

Descartes' Central Idea

Descartes' Doubts About Perception. Is What We See, Hear or Smell Real?

Descartes begins his famous book *Meditations on First Philosophy* from our normal everyday understanding of the world. All of us, says Descartes, initially take to be real and true the things that we see, hear, smell, touch or taste all day every day. In short, we rely, as human beings, in the first place on the evidence of our five senses:

Whatever I have up till now accepted as most true I have acquired either from the senses or through the senses.[20]

But it is precisely here that we must begin to doubt, because we often see something with our own eyes that proves later to be an optical illusion or a mirage. For example, if we plunge a straight stick into a pond in such a way that half of it is submerged and half not, the stick will, to all appearances, look broken in the middle.

But it is not really so at all; this is only the effect on our eyes of the refraction of light occurring in the water. And if, for example, we see the top of a church steeple glittering gold in the midday sun, it by no means follows from this that the steeple in question is actually made of gold. At evening, the same steeple may have a reddish glow, while on dull and sunless afternoons it may appear grey. But none of these three instances really give us any true information about its actual colour.

Descartes himself uses, in order to illustrate his doubts about whether truth can really be conveyed to us by or through our five senses, the example of a piece of beeswax. One might initially be of the view that a piece of such wax is something whose qualities it is very easy to perceive. It can be smelt, seen, touched; it even, if one knocks on it, appears to affect the hearing in one specific way:

Let us take, for example, this piece of wax [...] Its colour, shape and size are plain to see. It is hard, cold and can be handled without difficulty. If you rap it with your knuckle, it makes a sound. In short, it has everything which appears necessary to enable

a body to be known as distinctly as possible. But even as I speak I put the wax by the fire: and look, the residual taste is eliminated, the smell goes away, the colour changes, the shape is lost, the size increases. It becomes liquid and hot; you can hardly touch it [...].[21]

In other words, all those qualities and characteristics of the beeswax which we had initially believed were easily and surely recognizable through our five senses are now suddenly altered beyond all recognition. Another illustration of how little we can rely upon the evidence of our senses, says Descartes, is provided by our changing perceptions of the size of the sun. If we watch, from some distance, the sun setting over the sea it will seem to us to be a round ball of relatively modest dimensions. Even if we set this perception in relation to our perception of this same heavenly body at other times of day and consider the sun when it is rising, or standing at midday high in the sky, it will still appear to us to be a body that is relatively small in comparison with the perceived size of the mountains or other major features of the landscape and with our perception of the extension of the planet Earth as a whole. Even a whole series of observations of the sun, then, made at morning, noon and evening, can prove all of them to be deceptive:

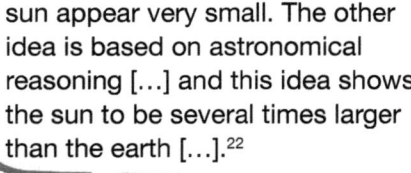

For example, there are two different ideas of the sun which I find within me. One of them, which is acquired, as it were, from the senses [...], makes the

sun appear very small. The other idea is based on astronomical reasoning [...] and this idea shows the sun to be several times larger than the earth [...].[22]

Descartes arrives, then, as regards our perception of things through our senses, at the following conclusion:

From time to time I have found that the senses deceive, and it is prudent never to trust completely those who have deceived us even once.[23]

But, so Descartes' meditations continue, perhaps it is only far-away objects that I find myself unable to recognize and know clearly and distinctly. What happens when I direct my senses not on something distant like the sun but rather on something which lies very close to me? For example, when I see and feel my own body, surely here I cannot be victim of any illusion or deception?

Yet although the senses occasionally deceive us with respect to objects which are very small or in the distance, there are many other beliefs about which doubt is quite impossible [...] For example, that I

am here, sitting by the fire, wearing a winter dressing-gown, holding this piece of paper in my hands, and so on. Again, how could it be denied that these hands or this whole body are mine?[24]

Descartes' doubts do indeed seem to have to come, here, finally to an end. Because it does really seem to be the case, does it not, that, if I find myself sitting, like Descartes, before an open fire, observing and experiencing my own body in the closest and most intimate way, while holding in my hand a piece of paper which I can also physically feel and move around, then there really can no longer be any question of doubting the reality of these things.

Descartes reply here, however, is: "No! If we are to be truly consistent, then we must indeed doubt the reality even of these experiences and of the things involved in them". Because even if we feel such a piece of paper between our fingers, and feel that we can move it back and forth, these feelings and sensations could, after all, correspond to no reality. It is always, for example, possible that we are, in reality, asleep and are simply dreaming it all.

Descartes' Doubts About Our Waking Mind: Is What We Experience Real or Could It Be Only a Dream?

Even when we are sleeping and dreaming we have, as is well known, experiences that feel extremely real. We see things, smell things, hear things, feel things and generally experience a great deal that proves, however, once we have woken up and examined the facts, to have been nothing but our imagination. How, then, Descartes asks, can we reliably ascertain whether we are in fact awake when we have the experiences we think we have or whether we are only dreaming them? Descartes describes how, in an attempt to assure himself that he is indeed awake, he moves his head back and forth as he sits in his armchair:

I shake my head and it is not asleep [...] All this would not happen with such distinctness to someone asleep.[25]

But he soon finds that the consistency of his logic compels him to admit to himself that even this experiment has been in vain and has proven nothing. Because, of course, these movements of his head are likewise something that he might have only dreamed:

How often, asleep at night, am I convinced of just such familiar events – that I am here in my dressing-gown, sitting by the fire – when in fact I am lying undressed in bed![26]

Even if, Descartes goes on to say, he were to pinch himself on the arm and cause himself to feel pain, not even this would really give him any assurance of being awake. Because we do in fact also have dreams which involve a whole mass of such things as colours, moods and yes, even feelings of physical pain. These feelings seem absolutely real to us. This is why we are so relieved when we awaken from a nightmare, or disappointed when some pleasant wish-fulfilment dream suddenly comes to an end. It has even been known to happen that people have dreamed that they were able to float suspended in the air a few inches above their bed.

They have even sometimes woken up, remembered the dream, and tried testing this newly-acquired ability in their waking state. The joy of those few people who, on trying to float once again, discovered that they could still do it has tended to be a short-lived joy, since not much time passes before such people wake up a second time, this time for real, and recognize that even the apparently "wide awake" experience of weightlessness had only been a second layer of dream. Descartes himself confirms the lesson of such experiences:

As I think about this more carefully, I see plainly that there are never any sure signs by means of which being awake can be distinguished from being asleep.[27]

We can, then, never be entirely sure of these things. Descartes, however, continues to sit in front of his fire in his dressing-gown meditating on the notions of dream and reality. He now casts a critical glance on his own reasoning up to this point and asks himself whether what we see before our "mind's eye" when we are dreaming is always necessarily untrue or whether, rather, there cannot be something real and true even in the state of dreaming:

Suppose, then, that I am dreaming and that these particulars – that my eyes are open, that I am moving my head and stretching out my hands – are not true

> [...] Nonetheless, it must surely be admitted that the visions which come in sleep are like paintings, which must have been fashioned in the likeness of things that are real [...][28]

Even in our most fantastic dreams, then, argues Descartes, we can only ever be combining in new and imaginative ways images, bodies, colours and scents etc. the models and patterns for which really do exist in reality. Even if we should dream of a winged horse, of which nothing of the sort, of course, actually exists in reality, such a dream nonetheless contains two real details: namely, the horse on the one hand and the wings on the other. Human beings, then, draw even their dream-images ultimately from reality. This is comparable, Descartes points out, to the work of artists who, for all the element of imagination it involves, also amounts in the end just to a rearrangement of certain things borrowed from real experience:

For even when painters try to create sirens and satyrs with the most extraordinary bodies, they cannot give them natures which are new in all respects; they simply jumble up the limbs of different animals.[29]

However novel or fantastic a world we may dream of in our dreams, then, we can never dream one that would lie entirely outside of the real world of bodies, forms, colours and materials. Nevertheless, Descartes goes on, the combinations into which these real elements are made to enter are indeed deceiving or misleading combinations. This, in the last analysis, is the reason why no science is entirely to be trusted which, like physics for example, consists in combining certain facts and pieces of knowledge regarding concrete bodies and concrete forms of matter. The results of such "sciences of composite objects", argues Descartes, are vulnerable, in principle, to the same deceptions and illusions, arising from the flaws of our five senses, as are dreams or the creations of art. But how does it stand with mathematics: a science which, in basic principle, requires no concrete colours, materials or specific bodily figures in order to perform its operations and is therefore not exposed to the risk of being misled or mistaken with regard to such concrete details? Surely this case of mathematics is different inasmuch as when I dream, for example, that $2 + 3 = 5$, or that a square has four sides, these propositions remain true whether they are dreamed propositions or actually enunciated and experienced ones:

For whether I am awake or asleep, two and three added together are five, and a square has no more than four sides [...][30]

For a brief moment it appears that Descartes has finally found, in mathematics and its related sciences such as arithmetic and geometry, that "absolutely certain" knowledge that he is searching for. Because arithmetic and geometry generate a knowledge which draws on pure logic alone and has, in principle, absolutely no need of any such perceptions as might prove to be distorted by a dream-state or the limitations of our senses. In contrast to the knowledge generated by physics, then, that resulting from the operations of these two latter sciences must be an absolutely pure and clear knowledge:

So a reasonable conclusion from this might be that physics, astronomy, medicine and all other disciplines which depend on the study of composite things, are doubtful; while arithmetic, geometry and

other subjects of this kind, which deal only with the simplest and most general things, regardless of whether they really exist in Nature or not, contain something certain and indubitable.[31]

Descartes' Doubts About Logic: Are We Victims of a "Malicious Demon"?

But Descartes does not rest content even with this insight into the seemingly special degree of certainty of the truths of mathematics. Because, as he continues to sit before his fireplace and meditate on these questions, he finds himself befallen by a terrible suspicion: perhaps even the axioms of our mathematics, that is to say our most basic assumptions as well as all the logical conclusions which are drawn from these, are nothing but one single huge error. Perhaps, so Descartes meditates further, we have been trapped since the moment of our birth in a world of total illusion which brings it about that all our thinking, right down to our most basic reckoning and calculating with simple numbers, is false. Perhaps, to use an image that long postdates Descartes but that certainly lies, nonetheless, in the descendancy of his 17th-century *Meditations*, we were born into, and live all our lives in, a kind of "Matrix":

Is there not a God, or whatever I may call him, who puts into me the thoughts I am now having?[32]

We should at least, if we are to be consistent in our project of doubting everything, not leave this possibility out of account. Because, if one or another sort of higher being really has played such a trick on us, then we do indeed need to doubt the validity even of our basic mathematical axioms:

I will suppose therefore that […] some malicious demon of the utmost power and cunning has employed all his energies in order to deceive me.[33]

Descartes recommends that we do indeed persist in our resolution of methical doubt even to the point of engaging in this strange thought experiment: that there might exist a *genius malignus*, or "malicious demon" who makes it his business to deceive us in all the affairs of life, and consequently lulls us into a false sense of security also as regards our basic principles of logic:

May I not […] go wrong, then, every time I add two and three or count the sides of a square […]?[34]

We are of course reluctant, Descartes goes on, to believe that an almighty God, given that he is also an all-loving one, would allow such a "malicious demon" to play tricks on us. And we are even more reluctant to believe that God himself could be, after the model of the "Demiurge" of the Gnostics, such a "malicious demon" and be himself responsible for so utterly misleading and deceiving us in all we think and do. On the other hand, however, great errors and delusions of this sort certainly have often occurred in the world. God, assuming He exists, undeniably has allowed the human beings He supposedly created in His image to be led into error again and again. For this reason alone, then, says Descartes, we need to take into account the possibility that such a "malicious demon" might exist. This may initially appear to be going too far but, says Descartes,

I know that I cannot (in fact) possibly go too far in my distrustful attitude because the task now in hand does not involve action but merely the acquisition of knowledge.[35]

If we suppose to be possible, to such an extreme extent as this, the operation on our minds of some "malicious demon", then we are obliged to doubt not only the truths of mathematics but basically everything which we encounter in the world and in our daily lives that has not already, in any case, been exposed to us as an optical illusion or a dream. That is to say, on this assumption, absolutely everything could be an unreality that we mistake for reality, as in the dystopian horror scenario of The Matrix. This means in turn that, in our search for some final certainty that can no longer be rejected as such, we need to take leave, thoroughly and completely, from all that we have been accustomed to feeling safe and secure in, throwing all these safeties and securities overboard. And it is indeed this uncompromising standpoint that Descartes now adopts:

I shall think that the sky, the air, the earth, colours, shapes and sounds and all external things are merely the delusions of dreams [...]³⁶

Indeed, not just "external things" but even one's own body must now, if we are to be consistent in this standpoint, be looked upon as very possibly an illusion, and one from which we are called upon to free ourselves:

I shall consider myself as not having hands, or eyes, or flesh, or blood, or senses, but as falsely believing that I have all these things.[37]

It is in such a state of nigh-dehumanized doubt that Descartes ends his first evening of meditation and finally goes to his bed. It is on the following day, however, that he achieves his epoch-making philosophical discovery.

The One Sure and Certain Truth: "I Think, Therefore I Am"

That Second *Meditation* of Descartes', which now follows, forms the centrepiece and key to all his notes bearing on his week of solitary thinking in his remote retreat. This one chapter of the six *Meditations* likely forms, indeed, the most often read and cited chapter of any philosophical book ever written. It begins with a personal confession:

So serious are the doubts into which I have been thrown as a result of yesterday's meditation that I can neither put them out

of my mind nor see any way of resolving them. It feels as if I have fallen unexpectedly into a deep whirlpool [...][38]

In this perturbed mood Descartes first lets all his doubts of the previous evening present themselves once again to his mind and exert once again their disturbing effect upon him. He reminds himself that he is now no longer in a position to trust anything he perceives through his eyes, nose, ears or organs of taste and touch, since these latter have proven to be deceptive. He also recalls to mind the fact that he can never know with any certainty whether he is awake or rather sleeping and dreaming. Thirdly, he even concedes to his own scepticism that those basic logical truths and insights known to him from arithmetic and geometry might also, in principle, turn out to be false, in the case where a "malicious demon" proves to have ensnared him in some Matrix-like web of false axioms and illusory calculative procedures:

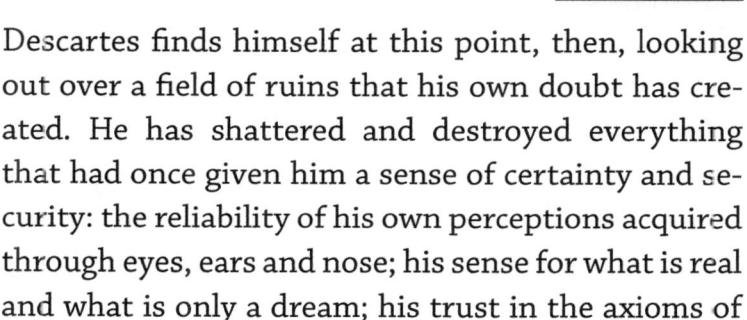

I will suppose, then, that everything I see is spurious [...] (that) I have no senses; (that) body, shape, extension, movement and place are chimeras. So what remains true?[39]

Descartes finds himself at this point, then, looking out over a field of ruins that his own doubt has created. He has shattered and destroyed everything that had once given him a sense of certainty and security: the reliability of his own perceptions acquired through eyes, ears and nose; his sense for what is real and what is only a dream; his trust in the axioms of mathematics; indeed, even his sense of the reality of his own body. For a brief moment, he entertains the thought that perhaps that absolute certainty that he had set out to find simply does not exist. But in this extremely difficult situation he musters the courage to consider, one last time, with his mind's eye the result to which all his doubting has brought him. He asks himself whether there is not, perhaps, something after all which has remained intact upon this great heap of rubble formed by all the apparent certainties he has cast into doubt. Astonishingly, he turns out not to ask here in vain. Suddenly, the scales fall from his eyes. The only thing that survives and remains is, paradoxically, that very "I" which had swung around it, from the start, that club of doubt by which everything else had been smashed and destroyed. Even were everything that I see, Descartes now realizes, to prove to be an optical illusion or a dream, and were the whole world around me to turn out to be some sort of *Matrix*-like simulation created by a "malicious demon", there would still remain, as an undeniable reality, my own self: the very self that doubts the reality of sense-perceptions and of the possible *Matrix*-world that these sense-perceptions compose. So much must hold true regardless of whether a "malicious demon" is deceiving me or not:

Let him deceive me as much as he can; he will never bring it about that I am nothing so long as I think […].[40]

Doubting is itself a form of thinking. And when I doubt, that is to say, meditate critically about anything at all, it matters not at all whether I do this in a state of wakefulness or in a dream. Because as soon as I doubt, it clearly necessarily follows that an "I" must exist that does the doubting:

So, after considering everything very thoroughly, I must finally conclude that this proposition *I am, I exist* is necessarily true whenever it is put forward by me or conceived in my mind.[41]

A thinking being can indeed, in any one of many ways, go astray in his thinking. But while he thinks and even while he goes astray, he must be in order to do so. The proposition must hold true, then, that

I am thinking, therefore I exist.[42]

To sum up, then: when I doubt something, regardless of whether it be when waking or in a dream, my doubting must be in every case just a special form of thinking. Thinking, though, is an undeniable expression of my existence. Insofar as I think at all, then, it follows logically and necessarily that I must somehow "be there". Consequently, the proposition *I think, therefore I am* is a proposition of a certainty that cannot be gotten around. Absolutely everyone who thinks knows with certainty, at least in the moment that he thinks, that he lives and exists:

And I found that this truth: *I am thinking, therefore I exist* was so firm and sure that all the most extravagant suppositions of the Sceptics were incapable of shaking it.[43]

With this, then, Descartes had finally found that "point of Archimedes" from which, he believed, it would be possible to understand, investigate and dominate the world as a whole:

I decided that I could accept it without scruple as the first principle of the philosophy I was seeking.[44]

And it is indeed by building on this first principle, namely that the human individual recognizes his own existence through the act of thinking, that Descartes develops his whole philosophical system. It is by no means the case that, by helping him to the knowledge of the "certainty of his own existence", the principle of doubt has exhausted its usefulness for Descartes. On the contrary, we find Descartes developing, in his book *Discourse on the Method of Rightly Conducting One's Reason and of Seeking Truth in the Sciences*, the four famous principles of "methodical doubt" which he proposes as apt to form, in future, the sole and sufficient ground and basis of all true scientific enquiry.[45]

Only when we follow four basic rules of method, Descartes argues here, can we be assured of attaining, through our reason, to sure and certain knowledge. Firstly, we must only claim to be true things which can be "clearly and distinctly" perceived. Secondly, in order to meet this condition of clear and distinct perception, we need to analyse every set of facts or situation we encounter into its individual component parts. Thirdly, beginning from the concrete thing, we should seek to know and understand these component parts both separately and individually and in their reciprocal effects upon one another. Fourthly, a list of the aspects of the problem at hand needs, in each case, to be drawn up which is so complete that no omission is possible. In Descartes own language:

The first rule was never to accept anything as true if I did not have evident knowledge of its truth [...] The second was to divide each of the difficulties I examined into as many parts as possible and as may be required in order to resolve them better [...] The third was [...]

to begin with the simplest and most easily known objects in order to ascend little by little, step by step, to knowledge of the most complex [...] And the last (was) throughout to make enumerations so complete, and reviews so comprehensive, that I could be sure of leaving nothing out.[46]

It is only, Descartes argued, by applying these four basic principles of methodical doubt that we can hope to arrive at truly scientific results in the way of knowledge. In order, for example, properly to judge whether global warming is a natural phenomenon or something due to human action we would need, according to Descartes, to follow precisely these procedures: i.e. first divide the problem into as many as possible individual parts and factors and then look at how these various parts and factors both operate in and for themselves and how they interrelate and interact with one another, while all along paying attention to the completeness and comprehensiveness of our considerations. In this particular case, in other words, detailed comparative investigation would have to be made both of the question of how the warming of the atmosphere occurs as a result of individual gases and of how this same phenomenon occurs spontaneously or is contributed to by specific human actions.

In order to "accept as true" the currently circulating hypotheses about global warming it would be necessary, according to Descartes, firstly to prove that the four different gases: carbon dioxide (CO_2), methane, nitrous oxide, and fluorinated gases are acting, singly or together, to seal off the atmosphere and, like the roof of a greenhouse, to allow the heat of the sun in but not out again, thus giving rise to the "greenhouse effect"; secondly, the emergence of these gases would need to be divided and analyzed into the specific individual states of affairs pertaining to each. Were these procedures followed, then the examination of the question might indeed yield the result, in line with the thinking of many "climate activists", that, although Nature itself produces to some extent, through volcanic eruptions etc., the gases in question, the mass of "greenhouse gases" is massively increased by such human activities as the burning of fossil fuels, felling of forests, and raising of cattle. But even once this complex configuration of factors had been examined and established it would still be necessary, according to Descartes, to draw up a proper comprehensive "enumeration" in order to make sure that all the relevant factors really had been drawn into the examination of the problem.

With this programme of methodical doubt Descartes wanted to set in motion a serious and careful investigation into the nature of the world and thereby to contribute to the progress of every individual science. He himself achieved initial successful results in the fields of mathematics and physics but regretted that, given the narrow limits set to an individual human lifetime, he could not hope to live to apply these principles to every single area of scientific endeavour:

But in order to bring the plan to its conclusion I should have to go on to explain in the same manner the nature of all the particular bodies that exist on the earth, namely, minerals, plants, animals and, most importantly, Man [...].[47]

But there arose out of Descartes' demand that that alone, in future, should be allowed to count as 'true" which had proven capable of standing the test of "methodical doubt" also a second major problem. This was the problem of the existence of God. Should this not also, according to the logic of Descartes' principles, be called into doubt? Descartes was determined, even in the face of this problem, to remain faithful to his principle of the primacy of rational thought. He undertook, therefore, the adventurous task of trying to prove the existence of God using only his new rational method.

If Thinking Alone Provides Certainty, Then God Too Must Be Thought of in Logical Terms

Also in his "proof of God" Descartes complies with the rule of scientific method which he has himself established whereby one should begin by separating and analysing each problem to be examined into its individual parts. With iron consistency, then, he dissects the idea that we have of God into its various separate "components". Because since time immemorial there have been associated with God a specific set of qualities or traits. According to a very widely shared idea of him he is

[…] infinite, eternal, immutable […], supremely intelligent, supremely powerful and (a being) which created both myself and everything else […] that exists.[48]

But this, says Descartes, is in the first instance just a notion or idea in our brains which cannot yet be taken to say anything about the real existence, or otherwise, of God.

Certainly, the idea of God, or a supremely perfect being, is one which I find within me as surely as the idea of any shape or number.[49]

All the ideas that we have in our heads, be it the idea of a triangle, of a tree, or of God, are, says Descartes, representations or place-holders or, as he puts it, "accesses through thought" to things and states of affairs. These ideas, however, do not spring into existence out of nothing but rather draw, in their very substance, on other ideas and primal images from which we derive or develop them:

When we reflect further on the ideas which we have within us [...] we see that [...] the greater the amount of objective perfection they contain within themselves, the more perfect their cause must be.[50]

Every idea, then, has a cause, and this cause must in each case be more objectively perfect than the idea itself. Descartes is drawing here, to some extent, on Plato's Theory of Ideas. When we see before us a round discus, a round clay dinner-plate, or a round silver coin, we can fairly assume that whoever manufactured these products was attempting to realize, as best they could, in all three of them the idea of roundness. In order to do this these manufacturers access the primal image, or original idea, of the circle. In this pure and perfect idea of a circle every single one of the points on the circumference is at precisely the same distance from their common centre. The person working in clay or in silver does his best, indeed, to bring this pure idea so far as possible to reality.

But the discuses, plates and coins which he produces necessarily deviate at many points more or less from this pure idea. They are, as Plato would put it, only imperfect copies of a perfect original. It is in the last analysis thanks to these perfect originals, or ideas, which, so Plato had argued, we have lodged in our minds ever since our birth, that we are able to recognize such distinct phenomena as a birch tree, an oak tree, a beech tree and a poplar tree as all exemplifications of the type or genus "tree". Their being so recognized and perceived is due to the prior existence of the common idea "tree" as a form or figure with roots, trunk, branches and leaves. Plato, indeed, goes even further than this: he suggests that the presence of the underlying or overarching "Idea of the tree" is the only reason why individual, concrete trees can even exist. The primal and original "Idea of the tree" has, he argues, its own reality and is the ultimate cause of all phenomena that bear this name.

Descartes indeed, for his part, does not see in the primal, original notions or ideas of things a reality of its own which exists all by itself. But for Descartes too the ideas of things, as causes of phenomena, are necessarily more perfect than their phenomenal "copies". Descartes also takes over from Plato the doctrine that all phenomena, notions and ideas in our heads have, in principle, a deeper reason and cause. For example, when I build a table, a house or a machine, the respective ideas of these latter things do not simply arise out of nothing:

For example, if someone has within himself the idea of a highly intricate machine, it would be fair to ask what was the cause of his possession of the idea. Did he somewhere see such a machine made

by someone else? Or did he make such a close study of mechanics? Or is his own ingenuity so great that he was able to think it up on his own, although he never saw it anywhere?[51]

But whatever answer the machine-builder might give to the question of just what cause he owes the idea which guides his building of his machine to, one thing is surely undeniable:

All the intricacy which is contained in the idea […] must be contained in its cause, whatever kind of cause it turns out to be.[52]

Just like the idea guiding the building of the machine, every other idea that we have in our head has a deeper cause. In the case of every one of these notions and ideas we can, every time, pose the question of the cause. This we should also do in the case of the notion or idea that we form of God:

Since, then, we have within us the idea of God, or a supreme being, we may rightly inquire into the cause of our possession of this idea.[53]

But when we begin to strain our minds to try to conceive of what still more perfect "primary idea" could possibly be the cause of our arriving at the notion of an almighty and perfect being, these strenuous meditations, Descartes argues, will avail us nothing. Because the idea of perfection is indeed an idea which cannot possibly be surpassed. Perhaps, it might be suggested, we simply spontaneously thought up this notion of God, prompted by a mood or a whim to do so. But this too, Descartes insists, can be ruled out as simply impossible, since we are ourselves just human beings and, as human beings, neither eternal, nor almighty, nor omniscient but rather mortal and burdened with many defects. There can, then, be no question of our having thought up the idea of God ourselves because if such were the case then something imperfect, namely Man, would have been the cause of something perfect, namely God, a thing impossible in basic principle:

For it is very evident [...] that what is more perfect cannot be produced by [...] what is less perfect.[54]

The idea, then, of God as eternal, infinite, all-powerful and all-knowing must come from elsewhere than from ourselves:

And since the supreme perfections of which we have an idea are in no way to be found in us, we rightly conclude that they reside in something distinct from ourselves, namely God [...].[55]

In the last analysis it is only God himself who can possibly be the cause of the idea of him that we find present in ourselves. Because only a truly absolutely perfect being is of a nature such as to be able to implant in us human beings that idea of perfection which follows necessarily from the idea of God. For this reason, argues Descartes, God must necessarily exist.

He also, however, has a second, additional argument for God's existence the structure of which can be traced back to Aristotle. If we proceed, as rationally-thinking natural scientists and believers in logic, on the supposition that everything in the universe follows certain regular laws and is comprised and bound within a network of interrelated causes and effects, then we are obliged, if we are to be consistent, to pose the question: what was the first cause of all? What was it that formed the very first link in the endlessly long chain of causes and effects? Such a cause would have to be a cause of a kind which needed no prior cause to bring it into being or, in other words, one might pose this question in the terms: what gave the initial push to everything without itself needing to have been pushed into motion by anything else? In Aristotle's own terms: who is the "Unmoved Mover"? Since we know that all living beings and all matter on this earth which displays any sort of bodily shape at all is necessarily subject to the physical laws of moving other things and thereby of being moved by them, it follows that the Unmoved Mover must be other than "bodily" and thus "not of this world":

Now, as far as the general cause is concerned, it seems clear to me that this is no other than God Himself, (who) in the beginning [...] created matter along with its motion and rest.[56]

To sum up, then: a cause, argues Descartes, can never be less perfect than its effect. Since, however, our idea of God is far more perfect than we ourselves are, this idea cannot have its cause or source in us but must have entered us from some place or being outside of us. The fact, then, that we have the idea of God within us leaves us no other logical option but to conclude that this idea was implanted in us by some higher perfection than our own, i.e. by God himself. With this, then, God's existence is proven. God is, by reason of his incomparably greater perfection, the cause of Man, and not vice versa. An independent existence of God, outside of our consciousness, thus reveals itself to be an indispensable assumption of all human thought.

This conclusion to the necessary existence of God from the fact of God's idea being present in the human mind is also derived, in part, from the so-called "ontological proof of God" developed in the Middle Ages by Anselm of Canterbury. The fact of God's existence is derived here from the fact that we conceive of him as perfect, since, so Anselm's argument goes, not to exist would be to lack a certain quality, namely existence itself, and thereby to be less than perfect. Descartes, in the fifth of his *Meditations*, illustrates Anselm's argument with a new example, saying that whereas I am free to imagine a winged horse, even though no horse is actually winged, it is inherently impossible for me to conceive of a perfect being who would be imperfect in the sense of lacking the quality of being real:

For I am not free to think of God without existence (that is, a supremely perfect being without a supreme perfection) as I am free to imagine a horse with, or without, wings.[57]

It has long since been generally recognized, however, that this supposed "proof of God's existence" advanced by Descartes is, in fact, a case of circular reasoning, or "begging the question". That is to say, what it sets out to prove is something which it secretly assumes to have already been proven. This is the case inasmuch as it conceives of the idea of God's perfection supposedly stored up in our heads as having, as one of its essential component elements, precisely the element: real existence. Clearly, if one looks on the very idea of perfection as something real, absolute and irrecusable just in itself, and supposes that the Perfect Being cannot possibly arise out of such an imperfect thing as Man, then it is indeed an easy thing to conclude that the only possible cause of the "real" idea of God the Creator is God's actual "reality", proceeding according to the motto: the Perfect Being exists because we are able to think of him as perfectly existing.

But Descartes' attempt to re-establish, through his "proof of God", that belief in the Creator which his philosophy of "methodical doubt" might otherwise have been suspected of shaking founders, in the last analysis, not on this "circular reasoning" but rather right at the start upon a still more fundamental problem. Because the fundamental nature of Descartes' characteristic approach to this key question, whereby certainty and reliability can be acquired through "thinking" alone and even God is a question one gains clarity about through thinking and rational meditation, was one which was, from the very start, irreconcilably at odds with the teachings of the church. It had been expressly stipulated by the Council of Trent (1545-1563) that all good Christians were bound to abide by the already-existing traditions of interpretation of Holy Scripture and of the proofs hitherto taken to be shown therein of the works of God in the world and thus to reject, for example, as untruths the new interpretations of these scriptures recently proposed by Luther and other Protestants. By Descartes' rationalism, however, no sort of biblical or scriptural interpretation, be it Protestant or Roman Catholic, is recognized to play any role in the pursuit of reliable knowledge. Scripture could no longer, for Descartes, form any basis for truth because none of the various biblical revelations, nor any of the miracles said to have been performed by Jesus prove clearly and distinctly knowable by the light of human reason, regardless of what specific religious interpretation one might give to them. Descartes "rational" proof of God's existence, then, was certainly not apt to shield him from the harsh criticisms of the church.

But it was necessary also for Descartes to derive from somewhere the belief in a good and all-powerful God in order for him to be able to go on with his *Meditations* at all. Because if there had persisted a doubt about the existence of a fundamentally benevolent God, and a concomitant suspicion that the world and its inhabitants might be the playthings of a "malicious demon", then there would have also to persist a doubt about whether a real world outside our heads existed at all. With the rational proof of God's existence, however, we have, in addition to the certainty arising through the fact of our thinking, now also the certainty that there is a real external world.

The Mind-Body Duality: Res Extensa and Res Cogitans

The result, then, of this *Meditation* consists in two certainties. Firstly, to the certainty that I am a thinking being:

Thought: this alone is inseparable from me [...] I am, then, in the strict sense, only a thing that thinks; that is, I am a mind, or intelligence, or intellect, or reason [...].[58]

Secondly, to the certainty that there exists, around me, a world external to myself:

The matter existing in the entire universe is thus one and the same, and it is always recognized as matter simply in virtue of its being extended.[59]

Descartes distinguishes these two regions or realms from one another as two fundamentally different substances which exist entirely independently each of the other. The universe as Descartes envisages it is a universe sharply divided on the one hand into mental, "thinking" substance, or *res cogitans*, and on the other into material, extended substance, or *res extensa*. As is indicated by the first of the two passages just quoted, these Latin terms mean, literally, "the thing that thinks" and "the thing that is extended". With "the thing that thinks" Descartes is referring to human beings, specifically to our mental, cognitive capacities; and with "the thing that is extended" he means all physical bodies which display an extension of some specific length, breadth, or height and thus prove capable of being measured. Examples of *res extensa* would be, for instance, the table at which we take our breakfast, the plates we eat it off of, the forks and knives we eat it with, and the bread and even the coffee that we actually consume. But the class of *res extensa* stretches, for Descartes, to comprise whole solar systems, plants, animals, and even Man's own physical body. This may seem at first to be a quite astonishing position to take because we human beings have a strong tendency to look on ourselves as beings "all of a piece". We find it very hard to adopt the stance that would, consistently, need to be adopted here: that of a mind sharply separated from its own body, or standing over against this latter as if against something strange and alien. This sense of ourselves as "all of a piece", however, is, in Descartes' view, mere illusion. Once I begin carefully and attentively to meditate on my own self I will begin very soon to recognize and understand what a difference there really is between my mind and my body and I will realize that these two things really do belong to two quite distinct worlds:

The first observation that I make at this point is that there is a great difference between the mind and the body, inasmuch as the body is by its very nature always divisible, while the mind is utterly indivisible.[60]

I can separate my body, through amputations, into many different parts. And it may well be that, after my death, bacteria and various other tiny life-forms may set about just such a work of dissolution and divide my body into many more pieces still. It is also possible for me, purely on the theoretical plane of the drawing of anatomical distinctions, to divide my body up into organs, bones, muscle masses and cardio-vascular system, something which is hardly possible in the case of my mind:

For when I consider the mind, or myself insofar as I am merely a thinking thing, I am unable to distinguish any parts within myself; I understand myself to be something quite single and complete.[61]

Between my physical body on the one hand, which might for example weigh 200 pounds and be five and a half feet long from its toes to the top of its head, and my mind or mental activity on the other there is clearly an essential difference, since I have an idea of this latter which is

[…] that of a thinking thing, which is not extended in length, breadth or height, and has no other bodily characteristics.[62]

Descartes, of course, does not deny that we have a physical body. It would be impossible to do so. But he emphasizes over and over again that the being of mind and that of body are two fundamentally different types of being. His sharp distinction, drawn in terms of their very substance, between *res cogitans* and *res extensa* leads him, in the end, to a very far-reaching conclusion:

> It is true that I may have a body that is very closely joined to me [...] But nevertheless [...] in so far as I am simply a thinking, non-extended thing [...] it is certain that I am really distinct from my body, and can exist without it.[63]

The mind, then, can exist without the body. With this, his idea of the immortality of the mind, or in other words of the immortality of the soul, Descartes places himself firmly within the tradition of Christian and of Platonic philosophy. Admittedly, there is raised thereby a problem which came to occupy a central position in his body of philosophical work. If mind and body really are regions of being as completely independent of one another as he claims they are, then how is the interaction between them possible at all? Put in concrete terms: when I form, in my mind, the intention of going to eat in the local restaurant, how exactly is it that I bring my feet to begin to move me in that direction? Descartes did indeed think in a very concrete and detailed way about the problem of just how our minds, in our day-to-day lives, succeed in taking up contact with our bodies.

He believed that he had found the necessary concrete "point of interface" here in the pituitary gland. This gland is situated directly in the brain. Descartes hypothesized that the pituitary gland was capable, therefore, of directly picking up a thought or mental impulse; it would then, as a reaction to this, produce a certain quantity of liquid which, once emitted from it, would in turn exert, through a kind of canular system, pressure on the nerves, for example, of the feet, by which these latter would be set in motion toward the destination, for example, of the restaurant.

Descartes conceived of the inverse process to this, or in other words such cases as that whereby a feeling of heat or pain would rise from the feet up into the brain or mind, as functioning in a, so to speak, "hydraulic" manner, as the following drawing, executed by the philosopher himself, illustrates:

To fully appreciate Descartes' thinking here it is useful to be aware that during Descartes' lifetime a sort of craze had seized the aristocracy of Europe for the embellishment of their private parks and estates with artificial waterways and other devices and constructions involving the control of water. Already in these early decades of the 17th century European engineers were in fact capable of employing water-pressure building up in communicating hydraulic systems in order to construct remarkably complex and elaborate springs, fountains and waterfalls on commission from these rich dukes and earls. Descartes suggested that the processes going on between brain and body could and should be conceived of on similar lines to these:

When the nerves in the foot are set in motion in a violent and unusual manner, this motion, by way of the spinal cord, reaches the inner parts of the brain and there gives the mind its signal for having a certain sensation, namely the sensation of a pain [...] This stimulates the mind to do its best to get rid of the cause of the pain.[64]

But not even these mechanistic descriptions enabled Descartes to offer a satisfactory account of just how the human body interacted with the human mind, given that he had begun by establishing such a total independence of the one of these "substances" from the other. "Cartesian dualism" has in fact remained a besetting philosophical problem during all the centuries since Descartes' initial advancing of his theories on this issue.

To sum up, then: Descartes' doubt leads him initially to one fundamental certainty, namely the certainty of his own existence as a thinking being. It is thought, likewise, which makes the existence of God appear to be a logical necessity. And from this in turn it follows that it is rational to suppose that the world created by God is not an illusory or deceptive but a real one. Building on these insights, Descartes eventually also acquires a certainty regarding the status of his own thinking self as a *res cogitans* which exists quite independently of all that which is material or corporeal, or in Descartes' own terminology all *res extensa*, in the world, including even his thinking self's own body. It is thinking, moreover, which enables us to become masters of the whole merely "extended" material world.

We must, of course, Descartes goes on, continue to

be sceptical about whether the world is exactly as it appears, to us, to be. Because we received, as human beings created by God, freedom as part of this creation, and with freedom also the possibility of being in error. "Methodical doubt", then, must be kept continually alive and must become and remain the foundation of every future science and form of knowledge.

Of What Use is Descartes' Discovery to Us Today?

A Short History of the Theory of Knowledge from Descartes to the Present Day

Of what use is Descartes' great discovery for us today? Does his famous saying "I think, therefore I am" still possess any real significance for us?

Whatever else can be said of it, the famous saying in question is certainly symbolic of the world's passage out of the Middle Ages into the modern era. Descartes' demand that truth be founded in some final certainty, unassailable by any doubt, which nonetheless did not consist in any form of religious faith or divine revelation certainly did, in an age of wars of religion like the Thirty Years War and persistent religious fanaticism, mark a bold turning point in human attitudes. One would not be wrong to describe it as a bidding farewell to medieval thinking. Like Columbus with his discovery of America, or Copernicus with his working out of a heliocentric model of the solar system, Descartes can be said to have opened up for mankind, with his rationalist approach to philosophy, an entirely new perspective on the world. Indeed, just as, in the history books, the beginning of the Modern Age is often dated to Columbus's crossing of the Atlantic in 1492, the date of the beginning of modern philosophy has surely to be set as lying somewhat more than a century later, in 1637, when Descartes first sets to paper his „I think, therefore I am". Descartes is the first to pose the question of how one can acquire a truly certain knowledge. In the age still profoundly marked by the religious ideal of "faith" in which Descartes lived, this was an act so revolutionary that it was surely with good reason that he lived in fear of being charged with heresy. Because, for the theologians who still had the last say in these early years of the 17th century, true knowledge is already given, and given alone, by belief in God and in the Gospels. It was this, as we have noted, that led Descartes to halt, at the last minute, the publication of his great cosmological treatise *The World*, after he received news of Galileo's condemnation on just this charge. It is speculated that he even, at this time, went so far as to destroy some of his early writings altogether.

His justified caution persisted so long that he published his second book, the *Discourse on Method*, only anonymously in 1637, even though he had quit, four years before, his native France for Europe's most liberal territory: the Netherlands. Descartes, in fact, moved residence some twenty-two times in his relatively short life, generally keeping his addresses secret from all but his closest confidants. One of the few men falling into this category was the scientist-priest Marin Mersenne, to whom Descartes wrote in 1630:

[…] I will always tell you my address, provided, please, that you tell no one else […] I fear fame more than I desire it[65]

For a long time, Descartes even considered the possibility that it might be wisest to publish nothing at all and to develop his thoughts in silence. Fortunately, this was not a resolution he carried out. His *Meditations* of 1641 brought him, especially when their original Latin text was translated into French in

1647, Europe-wide fame. In this text, he became the first thinker in Europe to dare to draw a distinction between the belief in "revealed truth" and rational knowledge. And not only this: in this work he also establishes, once and for all, the difference between everyday practical knowledge and true scientific insight. He repeats over and over again his demand that the rules he has laid down for the pursuit of true knowledge be consistently observed:

The first rule was never to accept anything as true if I did not have evident knowledge of its truth [...] and to include nothing more in my judgments than what presented itself to my mind so clearly and so distinctly that I had no occasion to doubt it.[66]

A little earlier on in the same text he writes:

It was always my most earnest desire to learn to distinguish the true from the false [...].[67]

Thus, Descartes became the founder of a whole new region of philosophical enquiry, namely, so-called "epistemology", or "the theory of knowledge". The themes of this new discipline were: "What is sure and certain knowledge? How does knowledge of external reality come to arise within our thinking apparatus? What role does sense-experience play in this? Can one know something independently of all sense-experience? What is truth?"

With his programme of radical doubt regarding all that we perceive through our senses Descartes sets in motion a discussion between "rationalists" and "empiricists" concerning just how we acquire reliable knowledge that was to go on for several centuries. The following centuries saw line up, on Descartes' own "rationalist" side of the argument, such figures as Spinoza, Malebranche, Leibniz and Wolff, while there opposed them, on the "empiricist" side the mostly "Anglo-Saxon" thinkers Bacon, Hobbes, Locke, Berkeley and Hume.

As the name clearly indicates, the "rationalist" current advocated a reliance on reason and reason alone. That is to say, they argued that true insights were to be arrived at through reflection and the drawing of logical conclusions alone. Descartes himself had already clearly formulated this position:

I now know that even bodies are not strictly perceived by the senses or the faculty of the imagination but by

the intellect alone, and that this perception derives not from their being touched or seen but from their being understood.[68]

It is above all his famous example of the "beeswax" that Descartes uses to show that the mere sense-perception of a thing does not lead to any real knowledge of it:

Let us take, for example, this piece of wax [...] Its colour, shape and size are plain to see.

It is hard, cold and can be handled without difficulty. If you rap it with your knuckle, it makes a sound. In short, it has everything which appears necessary to enable a body to be known as

distinctly as possible. But even as I speak I put the wax by the fire: and look, the residual taste is eliminated, the smell goes away, the colour changes, the shape is lost, the size increases. It becomes liquid and hot; you can hardly touch it [...] Yet the wax remains![69]

From all this, Descartes draws the eminently rationalist conclusion:

I must, therefore, admit that the nature of this piece of wax is in no way revealed by my imagination but is perceived by the mind alone.[70]

A modern example of how empirical perception through our five senses can mislead us is what we call "sunrise". The knowledge expressed in the verbal proposition "the sun rises every morning" may seem clear and indisputable, since we do indeed see the sun climb up over the horizon at the end of every night. But considered from the rationalist viewpoint, of course, the statement is false. In terms of what reason clearly understands to be the case, the only correct way of describing what happens here is to say: every morning the earth's rotation turns our planet toward the sun, just as it turns it, at evening, away from it:

[...] And reason convinces me [...].[71]

The decisive thing, then, so argued Descartes and the "rationalists" who followed him, is never the empirical sense-impression but always only the "truth of reason" behind it. Similarly, it is, in certain circumstances, false to state that someone is "tall" simply because the evidence of one's eyes reveals him to tower over others in the same room. Because in some other space, surrounded by other people, the same man might appear small. Again, what is decisive is not a perception but rather the thought that underlies it: in this case, the thought of relation and relativity. In other words, it is reason alone that can, as the logically comparing mental agency, decide whether something is "large" or "small". Likewise, it is reason alone that can decide whether the sun is really "rising" or whether we are merely being turned toward it by the earth's rotation.

The "empiricists" saw matters in exactly the opposite way to this. They held that it was not thought but rather experience, that is to say, the perception of the world through our five senses, that was the surest and most reliable source of all truth. The name "empiricist" is in fact derived from the Latin word for "experience", or "following experience". Though philosophers, they had little sympathy with "pure theory", teaching rather that one ought to examine the things of the world with one's own eyes and rely, in one's judgments, on experiments and on what could be concretely perceived. His passion for this experience-based method proved to be the downfall of one of its first and most famous proponents, Sir Francis Bacon. In the course of an experiment investigating the effects of freezing on meat preservation, he is said to have lingered too long in the ice-house, caught pneumonia, and died. This did not, however, prevent him from continuing to be viewed as the "father" of this great and enduring rival to rationalism as a philosophical method. In the eyes of his empiricist successors he had acted exactly as a philosopher should act, because knowledge about Nature and its laws is to be acquired, so these thinkers argued, primarily through the gathering of sense-experiences and sense-data. They were in the habit of comparing the human organism to a sort of empty barrel into which, from birth on, ever more images, impressions and experiences come to be poured. A very small child, for example, will have no fear of fire. But after its first occasion of being burnt it will not want to repeat the experience, since it will store away what it has undergone, in its understanding, as something "painful". "There is nothing in the mind that was not, before, in the senses," wrote one of the most famous of the empiricists, John Locke. That is to say, the empiricists, although they did not outright deny the existence of mind, saw it only as a sort of "storage facility" and not at all as the basis and foundation of knowledge This foundation, they argued, was rather empirical experience.

Descartes, however, for his part, gave precedence to pure thought over all experience. The triangle, for example, he pointed out, is a pure "figure of thought". A person can make logically recognizable and indisputably true statements about this thought-figure "triangle" even if he has never empirically seen or touched any triangular object in his life:

When, for example, I imagine a triangle, even if perhaps no such figure exists, or has ever existed, anywhere outside my thought, there is still a determinate nature, or essence, or

form of the triangle (of which) various properties can be demonstrated [...], for example that its three angles equal two right angles, that its greatest side subtends its greatest angle, and the like [...].[72]

Empiricists will object here that Descartes must certainly at some point in his life, even if it was only as a child in school, have seen a drawing or a wooden model of a triangle and that if he had not had these experiences he would not have been able to envisage the "pure figure of thought". But Descartes retorts here:

It would be beside the point for me to say that, since I have from time to time seen bodies of triangular shape, the idea of the triangle may have come to me from external things by means of the sense organs. For I can think up countless other shapes which there can be

no suspicion of my ever having encountered through the senses and yet I can demonstrate various properties of these shapes just as I can with the triangle. All these properties are certainly true, since I am clearly aware of them [...].[73]

Who is right here, the rationalists or the empiricists? Almost two centuries later, Immanuel Kant answers this question with a "neither and both". In order to categorize and form judgments, argues Kant, we require both these things: on the one hand empirical sense-perception and on the other the capacity of our mind to think. Every bit of knowledge we acquire stands, so to speak, "on these two legs". If either one of them is lacking, the act of knowing fails. If, for example, when we set about trying to "know" the piece of beeswax, the ordering power of reason is lacking, then the experience we gain, through our senses, of the state, sometimes solid, sometimes fluid, of this wax remains a confusing, chaotic, blind experience. The sense-impressions have been received, indeed, but they cannot be further processed. But if, conversely, we lack all actual empirical experience, all real sense-impressions, of the piece of wax in question, any thoughts or ideas that we may form about it necessarily remain empty, without real substance: "Without sensibility no object would be given to us and without understanding none would be thought. Thoughts without content are empty; intuitions without concepts are blind."[74]

Since Kant it has been recognized that every piece of scientific knowledge, indeed every item of knowledge generally, rests and relies, on the one hand, on the evidence of our senses or, in other words, on observable and measurable experiments and, on the other hand, on the correct application of our apparatus of thinking. Kant hereby takes his cue both from Descartes and from Descartes' empiricist critics in order to lay what was to become the foundation of the whole of modern science. The "theory of knowledge", however, has gone on developing to a point of sophistication even beyond this Kantian one. For the current "state of the art" of the theory of knowledge we need to look to the work of the Anglo-Austrian philosopher Karl Popper. In his major philosophical work Popper comes to the conclusion that even a theory which, in keeping with the demands of the Kantian theory of knowledge, would be both perfectly thought through and thoroughly supported by empirical experience, might, after a certain period of time, cease to be valid. Whenever, argues Popper, either the empirical facts change or some better explanatory model for these facts is discovered, a scientific theory which had up to that point counted as "true" will have to be replaced by a new and better one. The scientific proposition "all swans are white", for example, counted for centuries as a true one. But when, one day, black swans were suddenly discovered in Patagonia this supposed "truth" had to be dropped. Even that Newtonian physics whose principles had been considered, for centuries, to be indisputable had to give way and be replaced when Einstein, with his theory of relativity, proved able to make still more accurate predictions about the positions of the heavenly bodies.

Looked at in this way, we may say that Popper's new "theory of knowledge" opposes to Descartes' demand for clear and timeless certainty the sobering insight that there can, in fact, be no such thing, since no certainty can ever be anything but provisional. Every scientist must be aware that his theory will only count as "true" until some better model of explanation is found. If Descartes felt able, in the 17th century, to say

I now seem to be able to lay it down as a general rule that whatever I perceive very clearly and distinctly is true.[75]

Karl Popper speaks for more and more of us, today, when he claims that "even in the best and surest science we are dealing only with suppositional knowledge. Not with knowledge, but with suppositional

knowledge"[76] and that "scientific progress consists in finding out errors and in replacing these errors with something better. With a better hypothesis."[77]

The Success of Cartesian Dualism and Its "Dark Side": the Body as "Just a Machine"

Like many world-famous thinkers Descartes set in motion, with his philosophical discovery, processes with long-lasting consequences – some of them beneficial, others fateful. His dualistic distinction, for example, between, on the one hand, the *res cogitans*, or the thinking consciousness of the subject, and, on the other hand, the *res extensa*, or the world of soulless objects is a paradigm example of how a philosophical discovery can "cut both ways". Because on the one hand Descartes can be said to have given wings to the theory of knowledge, the very foundation of modern natural-scientific research, by posing the question of just how sure and certain knowledge, which can used to master Nature through technology, is achieved; on the other hand, however, Descartes' thought had the effect of pushing the human subject, as the one "thing that thinks", into the centre of the universe and degrading everything surrounding this human subject to the status of a soulless object of research. This philosophy, in other words, glorifies the absolute autonomy of the human subject. It sees the objects of Nature as things to be known, and through being known controlled, by the human mind. Descartes even hoped that it would be possible, through the nascent mechanistic physics of his day, to precisely calculate and control the changes in the human body, such as growing sick or growing old, as one might do in the case of some manufactured automaton.

This dualistic division, then, into *res cogitans* and *res extensa* applies not just to Man's relation to the inanimate world outside himself but also to his relation to his own body. We ourselves consists of the two "regions" mind and matter. This is something acknowledged in certain old biblical sayings still today in common use, such as "the spirit is willing but the flesh is weak" or in the modern formulation "work your body". Doctors too distinguish properly corporeal complaints from so-called mental illnesses, psychological from physical symptoms. The former are treated by psychiatrists, psychoanalysts and psychotherapists, the latter by physiotherapists, surgeons and general practitioners.

The great positive consequence of Cartesian dualism was a massive efflorescence of the natural sciences and the arising, all over Europe, of a new aspiration and ambition to finally unlock, in disregard of all the old religious pieties and ecclesiastical taboos, the mechanisms and laws of the cosmos and of Man's own body and to gain mastery over both:

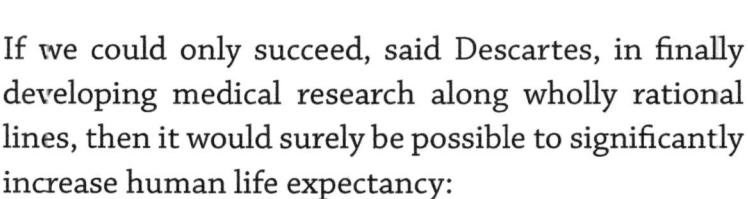

This is desirable not only for the invention of innumerable devices which would facilitate our enjoyment of the fruits of the earth and all the goods we find there but also, and most importantly, for the maintenance of health.[78]

If we could only succeed, said Descartes, in finally developing medical research along wholly rational lines, then it would surely be possible to significantly increase human life expectancy:

[...] We might free ourselves from innumerable diseases, both of the body and of the mind, and perhaps even from the infirmity of old age [...].[79]

Among the contemporaries of Descartes who carried out research in this way were Galileo, Newton and Hieronymus Fabricius. Galileo, for example, invented hydraulic mechanisms, along with some of the first forms of thermometer and telescope. The Italian surgeon Hieronymus Fabricius was just then acquiring, through corpse-dissections which had hitherto lain under a taboo, detailed knowledge of human anatomy, useful for example in the resetting of broken or disjointed limbs. Eloquent testimony to this is the following mechanistic diagram, ascribed to Fabricius, of the human motor apparatus, intended, it was said, for the repair of joints and "the setting of broken or displaced bones":

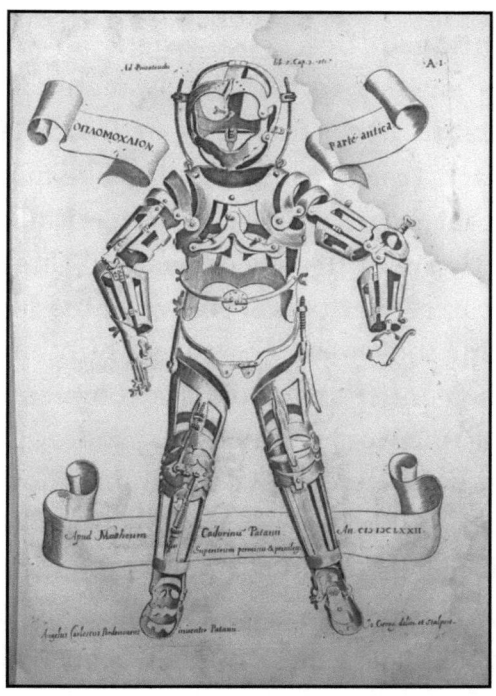

As Descartes had predicted, and indeed encouraged, the following centuries did in fact see groundbreaking progress in medicine, especially after the discovery of hygiene as the indispensable precondition for the success of operations of all kinds. We may certainly say, then, that Descartes gave wings, with his division of subject from object, mind from body, to modern scientific research.

But Cartesian dualism and its mechanistic image of the body also had their consequences for the relationship of human beings to other animals. As we have mentioned, Descartes assigns all animals except Man entirely to the merely material world of the *res extensa*. In contrast to Man, Descartes argues, animals lack a *cogito*; they function like mindless automata, that is to say, purely mechanically. They do not, strictly speaking, see or hear; all that happens, says Descartes, is that certain machine-like "seeing and hearing movements" occur within them. That is to say, their inner structure is a completely one-dimensional one. Some animals may indeed, Descartes concedes, occasionally give the impression of being clever and of having personalities, since they often display skills we do not possess. But this always proves, on closer examination, to be an illusion. Cats, for example, may, unlike human beings, always fall on their feet or may seem, in stressful situations, always intuitively to do what is right, while the reflective nature of human beings often proves a hindrance under such conditions. But

[…] Although many animals show more skill than we do in some of their actions, (this) does not prove that they have any

intelligence [...] It proves rather that they have no intelligence at all, and that it is Nature which acts in them [...].[80]

It is, then, not the cogito but rather some mechanism of Nature that acts here. It is this mechanism of Nature that automatically brings it about that cats are turned in the air as they fall and are landed squarely on all four paws. For this reason, Descartes compares that superior dexterity that we sometimes see in animals to a properly wound-up clock or watch:

In the same way a clock, consisting only of wheels and springs, can count the hours and measure time more accurately than we can with all our wisdom.[81]

In the end, argues Descartes, animals must be seen merely as well-functioning automata, like clocks. This idea, combined with the general craze for mechanics and other forms of technology setting in as the Scientific Revolution got underway, gave rise, at the start of the following century to the bizarre fashion of indeed recreating living animals in the form of little robot-like automata.

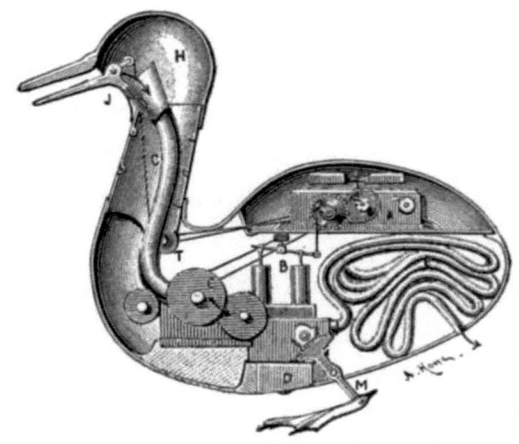

In 1737 the French inventor Vaucanson succeeded in constructing, out of more than four hundred movable parts, a mechanical duck. Once wound up, his duck-robot was able to reproduce almost all the motions and actions of the real bird: flap its wings, make quacking noises through a little built-in bellows, take water and seeds in through its beak, go through the motions of "digesting" these through a rubber gut, and even let fall "duck droppings" after the "digestion" was completed. Some years later, indeed, it was discovered that the most impressive part of this creation, the digestion, was in fact a "cheat". Vaucanson had secreted in his mechanism two separate containers: one which permanently retained the "digested" seeds and another which dispensed a pre-prepared mucus-like substance that counterfeited digestion's end-product, faeces. Even the discovery of this piece of trickery, however, did not diminish Vaucanson's fame as the first man to perfectly mechanically reproduce an animal.

This key idea of Descartes' whereby animals, as soulless automata, belonged firmly and exclusively to the realm of *res extensa* had far graver consequences, however, than just such isolated displays of grotesque and tasteless ingenuity as Vaucanson's. The major negative consequence was the encouragement of a deeply unethical attitude on the part of human beings to all non-human animals, whom Descartes' vision had reduced to the level of "things". Because, as we have seen, such "automata", for Descartes, cannot be said in any shape or form to "think"; they are simply lumps of matter. That animals lack the capacity for reflective thought, and therefore freedom of will, can be seen, Descartes argues, already from the fact that they cannot speak:

This shows not merely that the beasts have less reason than men but that they have no reason at all.[82]

His rigid assignation of non-human animals to the realm of soulless *res extensa* sadly does make Descartes a thinker who paved the way for the deplorable practice of treating members of other species like dead machines without feeling or capacity for pain. For many centuries after Descartes, indeed, animals were in fact treated like "things" under the law. In Germany, for example, it was only right at the end of the 20th century, in 1990, that the Civil Code finally dared to contradict Cartesian dualism and declare: "Animals are not things. They too enjoy the protection of special laws."[83] In Europe-wide legislation it took even longer, until 2009, to "overcome Descartes". The Treaty of Lisbon gives the commitment that, in future, "all member states shall take fully into account the demands of the wellbeing of animals as feeling beings."[84]

The Cartesian division of mind from matter, then, is decidedly a double-edged sword. On the one hand, it "gives wings" to the rational investigation of Nature, its mechanisms and its laws, thus promoting every sort of progress in material production and in medicine; on the other hand, it tends to demote and degrade Nature to the status of a mere object, and an object, moreover, to be subjugated by Man, through Man's calculating and instrumentalizing power of reason:

My eyes were opened to the possibility of gaining knowledge which would be very useful in life [...] through which we could know the power and action of fire, water, air, the stars [...] and all the other bodies in

our environment [...]and thus make ourselves, as it were, the lords and masters of Nature.[85]

This is Descartes' great hope: that human beings can rise, through the knowledge they acquire, to become "lords and masters of Nature". We should not, of course, be too harsh on Descartes here and recognize that he was a "child of his age" who, like his great contemporaries Galileo and Copernicus, could hardly help but be filled with an enormous enthusiasm for the new possibilities being created by the nascent natural sciences. The telescope, the compass, the printing press were indeed opening up entirely new perspectives for trade, travel and exchange of knowledge between nations. We may indeed speak already in the 17th century of a "craze for technology". But those consequences of a total human exploitation of Nature which are becoming all too visible today, for example climate change, lay, at that time, far out of sight in the future. Nevertheless, one can, indeed one must, look on Cartesian dualism at least as the fateful starting point for that massive empowerment of the human subject vis-à-vis Nature which, though initially inspired by the boundless optimism of the Enlightenment, has resulted in developments which give every cause for pessimism.

Today, we know that the goal of an unlimited "lordship and mastery" over Nature is a goal that needs urgently to be re-thought, since it has brought with it CO_2 emissions, the large-scale felling of the rain forests, the cruelties of mass cattle farming and mass animal transport, the harm caused by fungicides and pesticides and the massive over-exploitation of fossil fuels. What we surely need today is a human self-understanding that goes beyond Descartes and enables us to see ourselves rather as collaborator or custodian of Nature.[86]

Descartes' philosophy, then, represented the emergence of a deep rent in Man's perception of reality. The devout men and women of the Middle Ages had felt themselves to be organic parts of a world pervaded by God's will. Already before them, the shamans and pagan priests of earlier times had felt themselves to be tightly bound into the eternal cycle of Nature. But since Descartes we have lived in a world with the human subject on the one side and "objective" Nature, over against him, on the other.

The positive aspect, we may say, of Cartesian dualism and of its key idea, the cogito ergo sum, consists in its emancipatory effect of freeing thought from the tutelage of religion. By emphasizing that the final ground of all certainty is the *res cogitans* Descartes places, instead of spirituality, rationality on the throne of science and compels the human race to separate faith and knowledge, theology and philosophy, in a way it had not been called upon to do before. The closed cosmos of the Middle Ages is broken open and split, once and for all, into two parts. Descartes himself sensed what shattering consequences his revolution in thought was likely to have. He wrote to a friend that it would surely be better to publish his works only after his death, since publication was likely to be dangerous for him. The friend responded with a remark that Descartes could not help but find grimly amusing:

I could not help laughing when I read the passage where you say that I am forcing the public to kill me so that it can read my writings sooner.[87]

Descartes takes the joke, however, and builds it into an account of the manner in which he was living and working which must be taken very seriously:

To this I can only reply that (these writings) are now in such a place and condition that those who would kill me will never be able to lay hands on them [...]

and will certainly not see them for more than a hundred years after my death.[88]

Whether this exchange of letters may have finally prompted Descartes to publish after all we cannot say. In any case he did so and attracted, as was to be expected, the ire of the church. Two years after the publication of the *Meditations* the Jesuits in Paris held a public discussion of Descartes' works, without informing the philosopher himself. After several such procedures, and a series of merely local bans, Descartes' writings were finally, in 1663, "placed on the Index", or in other words listed as "forbidden works", by the Pope himself. In 1691 the king of France forbade that they be taught at any French school. Descartes, fortunately, did not live to see these bans. He died in 1650 in Sweden, where he was protected by his position as private tutor to Queen Christina from persecution but suffered badly from the cold and the obligation to rise early to tutor the queen. He had been his whole life long, partly for reasons of genuine ill health, a very late riser and it is said that the queen's forcing him to attend her and teach her at such unholy hours as five in the morning contributed to his early death, only a few months after arriving at the Swedish court, at age fifty-three.

The many years he had spent, previously to this, in the Netherlands had been marked by constant attacks from the side of the church and fanatical churchmen. The Protestant theologian Gisbert Voetius had accused him of atheism. Certainly wrongly, since Descartes, though a rationalist, was far from being an unbeliever. It was his firm conviction that it was only the material, *res extensa* part of Man, or in other words our bodies, that are mortal; only these disintegrate and pass away; matters stand entirely differently with our mental substance, the *res cogitans*, which does not pass away at all.

Is the "Res Cogitans" Immortal?

In a letter of 1642 Descartes writes to his friend Constantin Huygens that thought, being *res cogitans*, is something distinct from our body, which belongs substantially to the order of *res extensa*, in that *res cogitans*, for its part, is immortal. Human beings are not born, he writes, simply in order to live the best life they can on earth, to work, to eat, to drink, to conduct research, and to attain to a ripe old age in having as many positive experiences as possible. No, Descartes is convinced that our souls

[…] are destined by nature for pleasures and felicities much greater than those we enjoy in this world […].[89]

These greater joys and felicities, Descartes believes, begin for Man only after our life on this earth is over. He even believes that we will one day be reunited with our dead loved ones:

Those who die pass to a sweeter and more tranquil life than ours. I cannot imagine otherwise. We shall go to find them some day and we shall still remember the past; for we have, in my view, an intellectual memory which is certainly independent of the body.[90]

Descartes emphasizes here the immortality of thought. The intensity of this letter's tone shows that he really was convinced that we have an "intellectual memory" that will survive after death. But what did he mean by this? How should we picture the survival, beyond this life, of this "intellectual memory"? Descartes himself does not expand further on this idea, so we can only speculate. Did he believe in the survival after death of the personal genius of each individual? Or only in the survival of such an individual's thoughts in society's collective memory?

However one might answer this question, there can be no doubt but that Descartes is defending the principle of the timelessness of pure thought. The dead, Descartes says, do not really die. We encounter them again and again. "Encounter" them at least in the sense that their thoughts and deeds have become lodged deep in the memory of mankind and we who are still alive can "meet" our forebears in this form, even though they are long dead:

Reading good books is like having a conversation with the

most distinguished men of past ages – indeed a rehearsed conversation in which these authors reveal to us only the best of their thoughts.[91]

The thinking, the *res cogitans*, of the "most distinguished men of past ages" survives, even if their bodies have long since crumbled to dust. Thus, we still remember today Plato, Buddha, Alexander the Great, Confucius, Gandhi, Marx, Kant, Einstein and others who have left their mark on our "intellectual memory".

The philosopher Hegel developed this idea of Descartes' much further. Hegel argued that it was not only the stories, deeds and thoughts of the great men of the past that remained preserved in the "intellectual memory" of mankind but all the deeds and achievements, indeed, of all the people who had ever lived on this earth, both the "distinguished" and the "undistinguished". Because "the Spirit of the Age", as Hegel understood it, by which each age in turn is marked and formed, is not just the work of a few great personalities but rather the sum of all the efforts expended by all the people of the time. Every single one, argued Hegel, contributes with what he thinks and does to the collective memory of the age and every one, too, passes, on every level, his knowledge and experience on to the next generation. Thus, the minds and spirits of these people are preserved even if, in the following generation, a new "Spirit of the Age" arises, since this new one will build upon the old. For this reason, where Descartes speaks of an "intellectual memory", Hegel speaks rather of a "World-Spirit". We must accord, however, to Descartes the great merit of having been the first to reveal to mankind the tremendous power of thinking – and not just of any thinking but specifically of rational thinking. Hegel certainly accords him this much, writing that: "René Descartes is in fact the one who marks the beginning of modern philosophy, inasmuch as this philosophy takes thinking as its first principle."[92]

"I Think, Therefore I Am" – Why This Idea is Still So Relevant

Descartes urges us to stop simply believing, without testing it, that which others claim to be "truth" and which is taught as such "in the schools". Rather, he says, we should doubt and call into question, ideally from our earliest childhood on, all that we have learned and that is prescribed for us to learn. Only when, as he puts it, something appears to us "clear and logical" should we accept it as true. This is, in essence, a timeless call for critical thinking:

It seems that the only way of freeing ourselves from (preconceived) opinions is to make the effort [...] to doubt everything which we find to contain even the smallest suspicion of uncertainty.[93]

It is, of course, impossible in actual practice to doubt absolutely everything that we encounter. If only because of the massive amounts of information circulating in our complex world, we have no choice but to rely, unexamined, on certain knowledge produced by research. If, for example, we are taught, at school, Darwin's theory of evolution, whereby Man developed over millions of years from simple groups of cells and still displays a certain genetic affinity to his animal forebears, we are more or less bound to accept all this, at least provisionally, as a "given". Nor can we really take the time to personally check and examine all the information that reaches us every day from the media. It is salutary, nonetheless, to always keep Descartes' warning in the back of one's mind:

[...] never to accept anything as true if (one) did not have evident knowledge of its truth.[94]

Precisely in a "media age" like ours there exists a great danger of manipulated images, doctored statistics and one-sided reporting. One particularly notorious example is the speech given by the US Foreign Secretary Powell before the UN Security Council on 5th of

February 2003, in which he said: "The material I will present to you comes from a variety of sources. Some of the sources are technical, such as intercepted telephone conversations and photos taken by satellites. Other sources are people who have risked their lives to let the world know what Saddam Hussein is really up to."[95] Powell then went on to show the assembled representatives, and the world press, a whole series of photos and documents apparently proving the existence of Iraqi factories producing chemical and atomic weapons, with a view to justifying the US's war on that country, which duly ensued.

But once the war was over, it proved impossible to find any sign of these "weapons of mass destruction" in the now-occupied Iraq. Finally, Powell conceded that the "proof" had been manipulated material specially "prepared" by the US secret service for the global public, admitting also that the deception had been a "black mark" in his career. Had the material been examined more carefully the Security Council would never have been taken in by it. Powell had painted a convincing general picture of the threat but no single one of the individual proofs would have stood up to scrutiny. Neglected, in particular, had been the measure, recommended by Descartes, of

[…] divid(ing) each of the difficulties examined into as many parts as possible and as may be required in order to resolve them better.[96]

Descartes' demand, then, that we should doubt even that which we see with our own eyes and hear with our own ears is more relevant today than ever. It is indeed a fundamental demand of all philosophy. Democratic societies in particular must be ready to doubt at all times. Absolutely indispensable to democratic discourse is the testing of others' views and also the readiness to accept that one's own view is a fallible one, open to error. Whoever wishes to persuade others to change their viewpoint must be ready to change his own:

I know how much we are liable to err in matters that concern us and also how much the judgments of our friends should be mistrusted when they are in our favour.[97]

Readiness to doubt is absolutely necessary for an open society, as Aldous Huxley pointed out in his late sequel, in essay form, to his dystopian fiction *Brave New World*: "Philosophy teaches us to feel uncertain about the things that seem to us self-evident. Propaganda, on the other hand, teaches us to accept as self-evident matters about which it would be reasonable to suspend our judgment or to feel doubt."[98]

The readiness, then, demanded by Descartes to look at the world with curiosity and wonder but in a critical spirit, and to call into doubt everything that appears to us to be certain, is a challenge that persists perennially and is absolutely indispensable as the fundamental stance of the philosopher. Given that the world is becoming more and more unmanageably complex, it is very tempting to renounce or suspend all doubt and simply comply with the views proclaimed by one's rulers, by the media, or by the majority in one's particular society or country. Such a retreat into private life, combined with a passive conformity to all received ideas in the public realm, is, sadly, an often-chosen option for escaping the stresses and strains of doubt and of (self-)sceptical discourse. But Descartes warns us against taking precisely such a course:

Living without philosophizing is exactly like having one's eyes closed without ever trying to open them.[99]

Whoever goes through life with open eyes will never cease to philosophize:

I am a thing that thinks, that is to say, that doubts.[100]

Bibliographical References

1   R. Descartes, The Philosophical Writings of Descartes, edited by
    Cottingham, Stoothoff, Murdoch et al, Cambridge University Press,
    Cambridge, 1985, Vol. I, p. 111
2   Ibid. Vol. II, p. 12.
3   Ibid. Vol. I, p. 114-15.
4   Ibid. Vol. II, p. 16.
5   Ibid. Vol. I, p. 186. These remarks are from a letter written by
    Descartes to the translator, from Latin into French, of his 1644
    Principles of Philosophy, which he saw fit to use as the preface to the
    1647 French edition.
6   Ibid. Vol. II, p. 12.
7   Ibid. Vol. II, p. 16.
8   Ibid.
9   Ibid. Vol. I, p. 151.
10 Ibid. Vol. I, p. 193
11 Ibid. Vol. I, p. 127.
12 Ibid.
13 Ibid. Vol. II, p. 18.
14 This first work of Descartes bore the ambitiously comprehensive title
    Le Monde (The World). Almost the entirety of the physics expounded
    in it was Copernican and Galilean in nature and therefore too perilous
    to publish so close to Galileo's condemnation. It was finally published
    in full only a quarter-century after Descartes' death, in 1677.
15 The Philosophical Writings of Descartes, edited by Cottingham,
    Stoothoff, Murdoch et al, Cambridge University Press, Cambridge,
    1985, Vol. II, p. 3.
16 Ibid.
17 Ibid. p. 49.
18 Ibid. p. 11.
19 Ibid. Vol. I, pp. 142-43.
20 Ibid. Vol. II, p. 12.
21 Ibid. p. 20.
22 Ibid. p. 27.
23 Ibid. p. 12.

24   Ibid. pp. 12-13.

25   Ibid. p.13.

26   Ibid.

27   Ibid.

28   Ibid.

29   Ibid.

30   Ibid. p. 14.

31   Ibid.

32   Ibid. p. 16.

33   Ibid. p. 15.

34   Ibid. p. 14.

35   Ibid. p. 15.

36   Ibid.

37   Ibid.

38   Ibid. p. 16.

39   Ibid.

40   Ibid.

41   Ibid. p. 17.

42   Ibid. Vol. I, p. 127 (Discourse on Method).

43   Ibid.

44   Ibid.

45   The Discourse on the Method of Rightly Conducting One's Reason and Seeking Truth in the Sciences was in fact published by Descartes, under its original French title Discours de la Méthode, some four years prior to the publication of the Meditations, in 1637. This earlier text already contains his key idea, namely that Man is above all a thinking being, and a first formulation of his famous proposition I think, therefore I am. The Meditations on First Philosophy, then, published under his own name in 1641 are, purely chronologically considered, a later work. They can be looked upon as a sort of introduction to, and "phenomenological" justification of, his basic philosophical idea, or in other words a justification of it in terms of his own actual lived experience, added subsequently to the idea's initial statement.
46 R. Descartes, The Philosophical Writings of Descartes, edited by Cottingham, Stoothoff, Murdoch et al, Cambridge University Press, Cambridge, 1985, Vol. I, p. 120.

47   Ibid. p. 188. These remarks are from a letter written by Descartes to the translator, from Latin into French, of his 1644 Principles of

Philosophy, which he saw fit to use as the preface to the 1647 French edition.

48 R. Descartes, The Philosophical Writings of Descartes, edited by Cottingham, Stoothoff, Murdoch et al, Cambridge University Press, Cambridge, 1985, Vol. II, p. 32.
49 Ibid. p. 45
50 Ibid. vol. I, p. 198.
51 Ibid.
52 Ibid.
53 Ibid. p. 199.
54 Ibid.
55 Ibid.
56 Ibid. p. 240.
57 Ibid. vol. II, p. 47.
58 Ibid. p.18.
59 Ibid. vol. I, p. 232.
60 Ibid. vol. II, p. 59.
61 Ibid.
62 Ibid. p. 37.
63 Ibid. p. 54.
64 Ibid. p. 60.
65 The Philosophical Writings of Descartes, edited by Cottingham, Stoothoff, Murdoch et al, Cambridge University Press, Cambridge, 1985, Vol. III (The Correspondence), pp. 20-21.
66 Ibid. vol. 1, p. 120.
67 Ibid. p. 116.
68 Ibid. vol. 2, p. 22.
69 Ibid. p. 20.
70 Ibid. p. 21.
71 Ibid. p. 29.
72 Ibid. p. 45.
73 Ibid.
74 Immanuel Kant, Critique of Pure Reason, Cambridge University Press, Cambridge, 1998, pp. 193-4
75 The Philosophical Writings of Descartes, edited by Cottingham, Stoothoff, Murdoch et al, Cambridge University Press, Cambridge, 1985, Vol. II, p. 24.
76 Karl Popper in Die Zukunft ist Offen, Munich/Zurich, 1985, p. 50

77   Karl Popper in Karl Popper im Gespraech, 1990 interview with Die Welt.

78   The Philosophical Writings of Descartes, edited by Cottingham, Stoothoff, Murdoch et al, Cambridge University Press, Cambridge, 1985, Vol. I, p. 143.

79   Ibid.

80   Ibid. p. 141

81   Ibid.

82   Ibid.

83   German Civil Code, Section 2, 90a.

84   Treaty of Lisbon, Article 13.

85   The Philosophical Writings of Descartes, edited by Cottingham, Stoothoff, Murdoch et al, Cambridge University Press, Cambridge, 1985, Vol. I, p. 142-3.

86   Not all Descartes scholars believe this critique of the consequences of Cartesian dualism is justified. Dominik Perler, for example, in his book on Descartes argues that the philosopher's rigid distinction between thinking and res extensa is above all a matter of methodology: "The approach starting from the thinking 'I' is merely a methodical means to the establishment of a sure ground for knowledge. Once this ground is established Descartes goes on indeed to take full account of other human beings outside the 'I' and of other living entities." Perler, René Descartes, Munich, 2006, p. 259.

87   The Philosophical Writings of Descartes, edited by Cottingham, Stoothoff, Murdoch et al, Cambridge University Press, Cambridge, 1985, Vol. III (The Correspondence), p. 52.

88   Ibid.

89   Ibid. p. 216.

90   Ibid.

91   Ibid. Vol. 1, p. 113.

92   Hegel, Lectures on the History of Philosophy.

93   The Philosophical Writings of Descartes, edited by Cottingham, Stoothoff, Murdoch et al, Cambridge University Press, Cambridge, 1985, Vol. I, p. 193.

94   Ibid. p. 120.

95   The full text of the speech was reported, for example, in The Guardian of 5th of February 2003.

96   The Philosophical Writings of Descartes, edited by Cottingham,

Stoothoff, Murdoch et al, Cambridge University Press, Cambridge, 1985, Vol. I, p. 120.

97 Ibid. p. 112.

98 Aldous Huxley, Brave New World Revisited, Chapter 5.

99 The Philosophical Writings of Descartes, edited by Cottingham, Stoothoff, Murdoch et al, Cambridge University Press, Cambridge, 1985, Vol. I, p. 180.

100 Ibid. Vol. II, p. 24.

Already published in the same series:

Walther Ziegler
Adorno in 60 Minutes
ISBN 9783750460232

Walther Ziegler
Arendt in 60 Minutes
ISBN 9783752649031

Walther Ziegler
Buddha in 60 Minutes
ISBN 9-783-7543-5135-2

Walther Ziegler
Camus in 60 Minutes
ISBN 9783741227738

Walther Ziegler
Confucius in 60 Minutes
ISBN 9783753423128

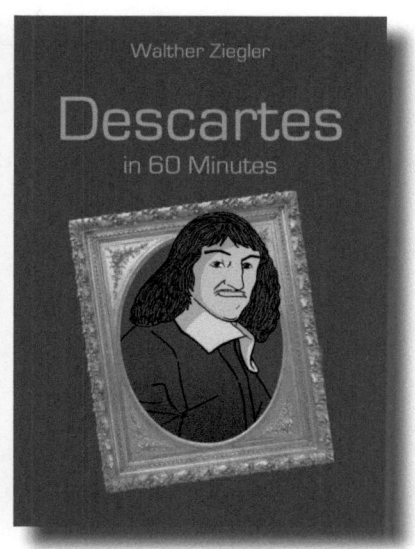

Walther Ziegler
Descartes in 60 Minutes
ISBN 9-783-7562-1316-0

Walther Ziegler
Epicurus in 60 Minutes
ISBN 9-783-7562-9515-9

Walther Ziegler
Foucault in 60 Minutes
ISBN 978375342688

Walther Ziegler
Freud in 60 Minutes
ISBN 9783741227707

Walther Ziegler
Habermas in 60 Minutes
ISBN 9783752612370

Walther Ziegler
Hegel in 60 Minutes
ISBN 9783741227677

Walther Ziegler
Heidegger in 60 Minutes
ISBN 9783741227752

Walther Ziegler
Hobbes in 60 Minutes
ISBN 9783751968317

Walther Ziegler
Kafka in 60 Minutes
ISBN 9-783-7562-9519-7

Walther Ziegler
Kant in 60 Minutes
ISBN 9783741226373

Walther Ziegler
Marx in 60 Minutes
ISBN 9783741227691

Walther Ziegler
Nietzsche in 60 Minutes
ISBN 9783752803822

Walther Ziegler
Platon in 60 Minutes
ISBN 9783741227615

Walther Ziegler
Popper in 60 Minutes
ISBN 9783750470897

Walther Ziegler
Rawls in 60 Minutes
ISBN 9783750424050

Walther Ziegler
Rousseau in 60 Minutes
ISBN 9783741227622

Walther Ziegler
Sartre in 60 Minutes
ISBN 9783741227653

Walther Ziegler
Schopenhauer in 60 Minutes
ISBN 9783750498853

Walther Ziegler
Smith in 60 Minutes
ISBN 9783741227721

Walther Ziegler
Wittgenstein in 60 Minutes
ISBN 9783750426955

THE AUTHOR:

Dr Walther Ziegler is academically trained in the fields of philosophy, history and political science. As a foreign correspondent, reporter and newsroom coordinator for the German TV station ProSieben he has produced films on every continent. His news reports have won several prizes and awards. He has also authored numerous books in the field of philosophy. His many years of experience as a journalist mean that he is able to present the complex ideas of the great philosophers in a way that is both engaging and very clear. Since 2007 he has also been active as a teacher and trainer of young TV journalists in Munich, holding the post of Academic Director at the Media Academy, a University of Applied Sciences that offers film and TV courses at its base directly on the site of the major European film production company Bavaria Film. After the huge success of the book series "Great thinkers in 60 Minutes", he works as a freelance writer and philosopher.